John Kember and Roger Smith

Viola Sight-Reading 1

Déchiffrage pour l'alto 1
Vom-Blatt-Spiel auf der Bratsche 1

A fresh approach / Nouvelle approche
Eine erfrischend neue Methode

ED 12956
ISMN M-2201-2569-0
ISBN 978-1-902455-79-2

www.schott-music.com

Mainz · London · Madrid · New York · Paris · Prague · Tokyo · Toronto
© 2007 SCHOTT MUSIC Ltd, London · Printed in Germany

ED 12956

British Library Cataloguing-in-Publication Data.
A catalogue record for this book is available from the British Library
IISMN M-2201-2569-0
ISBN 978-1-902455-79-2

French translation: Agnès Ausseur
German translation: Ute Corleis
Cover design by www.adamhaystudio.com
Music setting and page layout by Jackie Leigh
Printed in Germany S&Co.8213

Contents
Sommaire / Inhalt

Preface

Viola Sight-Reading 1 aims to establish good practice and provide an early introduction to the essential skill of sight-reading.

Sight-reading done individually is of little value unless the result is heard by the teacher. Ideally, sight-reading in some form should become a regular part of a student's routine each time they play the viola.

This book aims to establish the habit early in a student's viola playing. Of course, names of notes and time values need to be thoroughly known and understood, but equally sight-reading is helped by an awareness of shape and direction.

There are eight sections in this book, each of which gradually introduces new notes, rhythms, articulations, dynamics and Italian terms in a logical sequence, much as you would find in a beginner's viola tutor. The emphasis is on providing idiomatic tunes and structures rather than sterile sight-reading exercises.

Each section begins with several solo examples and concludes with duets and accompanied pieces, enabling the player to gain experience of sight-reading within the context of ensemble playing.

Section 1 uses open strings, first plucked then bowed, together with simple rhythms in 4/4 time.

Section 2 begins with open strings in 2-, 3- and 4-time before introducing the 1st finger.

Section 3 adds the 2nd finger, together with the key signatures of C, G and D major.

Section 4 adds the 3rd finger and the key of A major. The use of quavers (eighth notes) is introduced in simple time.

Section 5 introduces the keys of F, B♭ and E♭ major.

Section 6 introduces keys of C, G and D minor and adds both dotted rhythms and slurs.

Section 7 uses all keys so far introduced, both major and minor, and adds quavers in 3/8 time and open string shifts.

Section 8 concludes book 1 and is devoted to compound time, both 6/8 and 9/8.

To the pupil: why sight-reading?

When you are faced with a new piece and asked to play it, whether at home, in a lesson, or in an exam or audition, there is no one there to help you – except yourself! Sight-reading tests your ability to read the time and notes correctly, and to observe the phrasing and dynamics quickly.

The aim of this book is to help you to teach yourself. The book gives guidance on what to look for and how best to prepare in a very short time by observing the time and key signatures, the shape of the melody, and the marks of expression. These short pieces progress gradually to help you to build up your confidence and observation and enable you to sight-read accurately. At the end of each section there are duets to play with your teacher or friends plus pieces with piano accompaniment which will test your ability to sight-read whilst something else is going on. This is a necessary skill when playing with a band, orchestra or other ensemble.

If you sight-read something every time you play your viola you will be amazed how much better you will become. Remember, if you can sight-read most of the tunes you are asked to learn you will be able to concentrate on the 'tricky bits' and complete them quickly.

Think of the tunes in this book as 'mini-pieces', and try to learn them quickly and correctly. Then when you are faced with real sight-reading you will be well equipped to succeed on a first attempt.

You are on your own now!

Préface

Le propos de ce recueil de déchiffrage pour l'alto est de fournir une première initiation et un entraînement solide aux principes de la lecture à vue.

Le déchiffrage pratiqué seul ne présente pas grand intérêt à moins d'être supervisé par le maître. L'idéal serait que le déchiffrage prenne régulièrement place dans la routine de travail de l'élève à chaque fois qu'il prend son alto.

L'objectif est ici d'établir l'habitude de la lecture à vue très tôt dans l'étude de l'alto. Le déchiffrage suppose, bien sûr, que les noms et les valeurs de notes soient complètement assimilés et compris mais il s'appuie également sur la reconnaissance des contours et de la direction.

Ce volume comporte huit sections correspondant à l'introduction graduelle de notes, de rythmes, de phrasés, de nuances et de termes italiens nouveaux selon la progression logique rencontrée dans une méthode d'alto pour débutant. La démarche consiste à fournir des airs et des structures idiomatiques propres à l'alto de préférence à de stériles exercices de déchiffrage.

Chaque section débute par plusieurs exemples de solos et se termine par des duos et des pièces accompagnées afin de familiariser l'altiste avec l'expérience de la lecture à vue dans le cadre d'une exécution collective.

La section 1 recourt aux cordes à vide, tout d'abord pincées puis jouées avec l'archet, et aux rythmes simples dans une mesure à 4/4.

La section 2 débute par les cordes à vide et des mesures à 2, 3 et 4 temps avant d'introduire le premier doigt.

La section 3 ajoute le deuxième doigt et les armures des tonalités de *do* majeur, *sol* majeur et *ré* majeur.

La section 4 ajoute le troisième doigt et la tonalité de *la* majeur. Les croches y apparaissent dans des mesures simples.

La section 5 introduit les tonalités de *fa* majeur, *si*♭ majeur et *mi*♭ majeur.

La section 6 introduit les tonalités de *do* mineur, *sol* mineur et *ré* mineur et ajoute les rythmes pointés et les liaisons de phrasé.

La section 7 reprend toutes les tonalités déjà rencontrées et introduit la battue d'une croche par temps dans la mesure à 3/8 et les déplacements sur cordes à vide.

La section 8 qui conclut le volume 1, se concentre sur les mesures composées à 6/8 et à 9/8.

A l'élève : Pourquoi le déchiffrage ?

Lorsque vous vous trouvez face à un nouveau morceau que l'on vous demande de jouer, que ce soit chez vous, pendant une leçon ou lors d'un examen ou d'une audition, personne d'autre ne peut vous aider que vous-même ! Le déchiffrage met à l'épreuve votre capacité à lire correctement les rythmes et les notes et à observer rapidement le phrasé et les nuances.

Ce recueil se propose de vous aider à vous entraîner vous-même. Il vous oriente sur ce que vous devez repérer et sur la meilleure manière de vous préparer en un laps de temps très court en sachant observer les indications de mesure et l'armure de la clef, les contours de la mélodie et les indications expressives. Ces pièces brèves, en progressant par étapes, vous feront prendre de l'assurance, aiguiseront vos observations et vous permettront de lire à vue avec exactitude et aisance. A la fin de chaque section figurent des duos que vous pourrez jouer avec votre professeur ou des amis et des morceaux avec accompagnement de piano qui mettront à l'épreuve votre capacité de déchiffrage pendant que se déroule une autre partie. Celle-ci est indispensable pour jouer dans un groupe, un orchestre ou un ensemble.

Vous serez surpris de vos progrès si vous déchiffrez une pièce à chaque fois que vous vous mettez à l'alto. N'oubliez pas que si vous êtes capable de lire à vue la plupart des morceaux que vous allez étudier, vous pourrez vous concentrer sur les passages difficiles et les assimiler plus vite.

Considérez ces pages comme des « mini-morceaux » et essayez de les apprendre rapidement et sans erreur de manière à ce que, devant un véritable déchiffrage, vous soyez bien armé pour réussir dès la première lecture.

Vous êtes désormais seul !

Vorwort

Vom-Blatt-Spiel auf der Bratsche 1 möchte zu einer guten Übetechnik verhelfen und frühzeitig für die Einführung der grundlegenden Fähigkeit des Blatt-Spiels sorgen.

Vom-Blatt-Spiel alleine zu üben hat wenig Sinn, wenn das Ergebnis nicht vom Lehrer überprüft wird. Idealerweise sollte das Vom-Blatt-Spiel in irgendeiner Form ein regelmäßiger Bestandteil des Übens werden.

Dieses Buch hat zum Ziel, bereits von Anfang an diese Gewohnheit im Bratschenspiel des Schülers zu verankern. Natürlich muss man die Notennamen und Notenwerte komplett kennen und verstanden haben, aber genauso wird das Vom-Blatt-Spiel durch das Bewusstsein für Form und Richtung unterstützt.

Das Buch enthält acht Teile, die nach und nach neue Noten, Rhythmen, Artikulation, Dynamik und italienische Begriffe in einer logischen Abfolge einführen – ganz ähnlich, wie man es in einer Bratschenschule für Anfänger auch finden würde. Der Schwerpunkt liegt mehr auf dem Bereitstellen passender Melodien und Strukturen als auf sterilen Blatt-Spiel Übungen.

Jeder Teil beginnt mit einigen Solobeispielen und endet mit Duetten und begleiteten Stücken, damit man auch beim Zusammenspiel mit anderen Erfahrungen mit dem Blattspiel sammeln kann.

Teil 1 verwendet nur leere Saiten, erst gezupft, dann gestrichen, zusammen mit einfachen Rhythmen im 4/4-Takt.

Teil 2 beginnt mit leeren Saiten im 2/4-, 3/4- und 4/4-Takt, bevor der erste Finger hinzugenommen wird.

Teil 3 fügt den zweiten Finger hinzu, zusammen mit den Vorzeichen für C-, G- und D-Dur.

Teil 4 verwendet den dritten Finger und die Tonart A-Dur. Der Gebrauch von Achtelnoten in einfachen Taktarten wird eingeführt.

Teil 5 führt die Tonarten F-, B- und Es-Dur ein.

Teil 6 führt die Tonarten c-, g- und d-Moll ein. Hinzu kommen punktierte Rhythmen und Bindungen.

Teil 7 verwendet alle Vorzeichen, die bisher eingeführt wurden, Dur und Moll. Außerdem kommen Achtelnoten im 3/8-Takt sowie Lagenwechsel hinzu.

Teil 8 beschließt Band 1 und widmet sich den zusammengesetzten Taktarten – sowohl dem 6/8- als auch dem 9/8-Takt.

An den Schüler: Warum Vom-Blatt-Spiel?

Wenn du dich einem neuen Musikstück gegenüber siehst und gebeten wirst, es zu spielen, egal, ob zu Hause, im Unterricht, in einem Examen oder einem Vorspiel, gibt es niemanden, der dir helfen kann – nur du selbst! Das Blatt-Spiel testet die Fähigkeit, die Taktart und die Noten richtig zu lesen sowie Phrasierungen und Dynamik schnell zu erfassen.

Ziel dieses Buches ist es, dir beim Selbstunterricht behilflich zu sein. Das Buch zeigt dir, worauf du achten sollst und wie du dich in sehr kurzer Zeit am besten vorbereitest. Das tust du, indem du dir Takt- und Tonart sowie den Verlauf der Melodie und die Ausdruckszeichen genau anschaust. Die kurzen Musikstücke steigern sich allmählich, um zum einen dein Vertrauen und deine Beobachtungsgabe aufzubauen, zum anderen auch, um dich dazu zu befähigen, exakt vom Blatt zu spielen. Am Ende jeden Teils stehen Duette, die du mit deinem Lehrer oder deinen Freunden spielen kannst. Außerdem gibt es Stücke mit Klavierbegleitung, die deine Fähigkeit im Blatt-Spiel überprüfen, während gleichzeitig etwas anderes abläuft. Das ist eine wesentliche Fähigkeit, wenn man mit einer Band, einem Orchester oder einer anderen Musikgruppe zusammenspielt.

Wenn du jedes Mal, wenn du Bratsche spielst, auch etwas vom Blatt spielst, wirst du überrascht sein, wie sehr du dich verbesserst. Denke daran: wenn du die meisten Melodien, die du spielen sollst, vom Blatt spielen kannst, kannst du dich auf die „schwierigen Teile" konzentrieren und diese viel schneller beherrschen.

Stelle dir die Melodien in diesem Buch als „Ministücke" vor und versuche, sie schnell und korrekt zu lernen. Wenn du dann wirklich vom Blatt spielen musst, wirst du bestens ausgerüstet sein, um gleich beim ersten Versuch erfolgreich zu sein.

Jetzt bist du auf dich selbst gestellt!

Section 1 – Open strings
Section 1 – Cordes à vide
Teil 1 – Leere Saiten

Three steps to success

1. **Look at the top number of the time signature (4)**. It shows the number of beats in each bar. Tap (clap, sing or play on one note) the rhythm, feeling the pulse throughout. Count at least one bar of the time signature in your head to set up the pulse before you tap or play.

2. **Look for patterns**. While tapping the rhythm, look at the melodic shape and notice movement by step, skips, repeated notes and sequences (short repeated melodic phrases which often rise or fall by step).

3. **Keep going**. Remember, a wrong note or rhythm can be corrected the next time you play it. If you stop, you have doubled the mistake!

Trois étapes vers la réussite

1. **Observez le chiffre supérieur de l'indication de mesure (4)**. Il indique le nombre de pulsations contenues par mesure. Frappez (dans les mains, chantez ou jouez sur une seule note) le rythme tout en maintenant une pulsation intérieure constante. Comptez mentalement au moins une mesure complète pour installer la pulsation avant de frapper ou de jouer chaque pièce.

2. **Repérez les motifs**. Tout en frappant le rythme, observez les contours de la mélodie et relevez les mouvements par degrés, les sauts d'intervalles, les notes répétées et les séquences (courtes phrases mélodiques répétées progressant généralement par degrés ascendants ou descendants).

3. **Ne vous arrêtez pas**. N'oubliez pas que vous pourrez corriger une fausse note ou un rythme inexact la prochaine fois que vous jouerez. En vous interrompant, vous doublez la faute !

Drei Schritte zum Erfolg

1. **Schaue dir die obere Zahl der Taktangabe an (4)**. Diese zeigt die Anzahl der Schläge in einem Takt an. Schlage (klatsche, singe oder spiele auf einer Note) den Rhythmus, wobei du immer das Metrum spürst. Zähle mindestens einen Takt lang die Taktangabe im Kopf, um das Metrum zu verinnerlichen, bevor du klopfst oder spielst.

2. **Achte auf Muster**. Schaue dir die melodische Form an, während du den Rhythmus schlägst und achte auf Bewegungen in Schritten oder Sprüngen, sich wiederholende Noten und Sequenzen (kurze, sich wiederholende melodische Phrasen, die oft schrittweise ansteigen oder abfallen).

3. **Spiele immer weiter**. Denke daran: eine falsche Note oder ein falscher Rhythmus kann beim nächsten Mal korrigiert werden. Wenn du aber aufhörst zu spielen, verdoppelst du den Fehler!

Section 1 – Open strings
Section 1 – Cordes à vide
Teil 1 – Leere Saiten

Open strings.   Cordes à vide.   Leere Saiten.

1.

pizz. / arco

2.

pizz. / arco

3.

pizz. / arco

4.

pizz. / arco

Open strings – mixed.   Cordes à vide mélangées.   Verschiedene leere Saiten.

5.

pizz. / arco

6.

pizz. / arco

Open strings – change of rhythm.   Cordes à vide – changement de rythme.   Leere Saiten – Rhythmuswechsel.

10

15.
pizz. / arco

16.
pizz. / arco

17.
pizz. / arco

18.
pizz. / arco

Note against note.   Note contre note.   Erstes Zusammenspiel.

19.
Pupil / Elève / Schüler

Teacher / Professeur / Lehrer

20.

21.

Independent rhythms. Rythmes indépendants. Erweitertes Zusammenspiel.

22.

23.

24.

25.

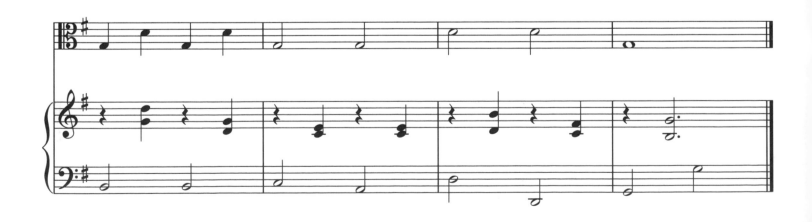

26.

27.

Section 2 – Open strings in 2-, 3- and 4-time
Section 2 – Cordes à vide dans des mesures à 2, 3 et 4 temps
Teil 2 – Leere Saiten im 2/4-, 3/4- und 4/4-Takt

Four steps to success

1. **Look at the top number of the key signature (2, 3 or 4)**. It shows the number of beats in each bar. Tap (clap, sing or play on one note) the rhythm, feeling the pulse throughout. Count at least one bar of the time signature in your head to set up the pulse before you tap or play.

2. **Look for patterns**. While tapping the rhythm, look at the melodic shape and notice movement by step, skips, repeated notes and sequences (a short repeated melodic phrases which usually riss or fall by step).

3. **Spot the 1st fingers** and make sure that you know the name of each new note.

4. **Keep going**. Remember, a wrong note or rhythm can be corrected the next time you play it. If you stop you have doubled the mistake!

Quatre étapes vers la réussite

1. **Observez le chiffre supérieur de l'indication de mesure (2, 3 ou 4)**. Il indique le nombre de pulsations contenues par mesure. Frappez (dans les mains, chantez ou jouez sur une seule note) le rythme tout en maintenant une pulsation intérieure constante. Comptez mentalement au moins une mesure pour installer la pulsation avant de frappez ou de jouer chaque pièce.

2. **Repérez les motifs**. Tout en frappant le rythme, observez les contours de la mélodie et relevez les mouvements par degrés, les sauts d'intervalles, les notes répétées ou les séquences.

3. **Repérez la première position des doigts** et assurez-vous de connaître le nom de chaque nouvelle note.

4. **Ne vous arrêtez pas**. N'oubliez pas que vous pourrez corriger une fausse note ou un rythme inexact la prochaine fois que vous jouerez. En vous interrompant, vous doublez la faute !

Vier Schritte zum Erfolg

1. **Schaue dir die obere Zahl der Taktangabe an (2, 3 oder 4)**. Diese zeigt die Anzahl der Schläge in einem Takt an. Schlage (klatsche, singe oder spiele auf einer Note) den Rhythmus, wobei du immer das Metrum spürst. Zähle mindestens einen Takt lang die Taktangabe im Kopf, um das Metrum zu verinnerlichen, bevor du klopfst oder spielst.

2. **Achte auf Muster**. Schaue dir die melodische Form an, während du den Rhythmus schlägst und achte auf Bewegungen in Schritten oder Sprüngen, sich wiederholende Noten und Sequenzen (kurze, sich wiederholende melodische Phrasen, die oft schrittweise ansteigen oder abfallen).

3. **Suche die Noten, bei denen du den 1. Finger brauchst** und versichere dich, dass du die Namen jeder neuen Note weißt.

4. **Spiele immer weiter**. Denke daran: eine falsche Note oder ein falscher Rhythmus kann beim nächsten Mal korrigiert werden. Wenn du aber aufhörst zu spielen, verdoppelst du den Fehler!

Terms and performance directions used in the accompanied pieces:
(You may note all directions and translations on the glossary page at the back of the book.)

Indications d'exécution utilisées dans les pièces accompagnées :
(Vous pourrez noter toutes les indications et leur traduction sur la page de glossaire en fin de volume.)

Begriffe und Vortragsangaben, die bei den begleiteten Stücken verwendet werden:
(Du kannst dir alle Angaben und ihre Übersetzungen in der Anhangseite hinten im Buch notieren.)

Andante	at a walking pace	allant	gehend
Con moto	with vigour	avec force	mit Energie
Waltz	a lively dance in 3-time	danse à trois temps	ein lebhafter Tanz im 3er-Takt

Section 2 – Open strings in 2-, 3- and 4-time

Section 2 – Cordes à vide dans des mesures à 2, 3 et
4 temps

Teil 2 – Leere Saiten im 2/4-, 3/4- und 4/4-Takt

16

Introducing the 1st finger.   Introduction du 1er doigt.   Einführung des 1. Fingers.

Both parts may be played by the pupil or pupils.

Les deux parties peuvent être jouées par l'élève ou par deux élèves.

Beide Stimmen können von Schüler und Lehrer oder von zwei Schülern gespielt werden.

48.

49.

50.

51.

52.

53.

This piece begins on the third beat of the bar in 3-time.
Count 1 2 3 1 2 before you begin.

Cette pièce débute sur le 3e temps d'une mesure à 3 temps.
Comptez 1, 2, 3, 1, 2, avant de commencer.

Dieses Stück beginnt auf dem dritten Schlag in einem 3/4-Takt.
Zähle 1 2 3 1 2 vor, bevor du anfängst.

54.

Andante

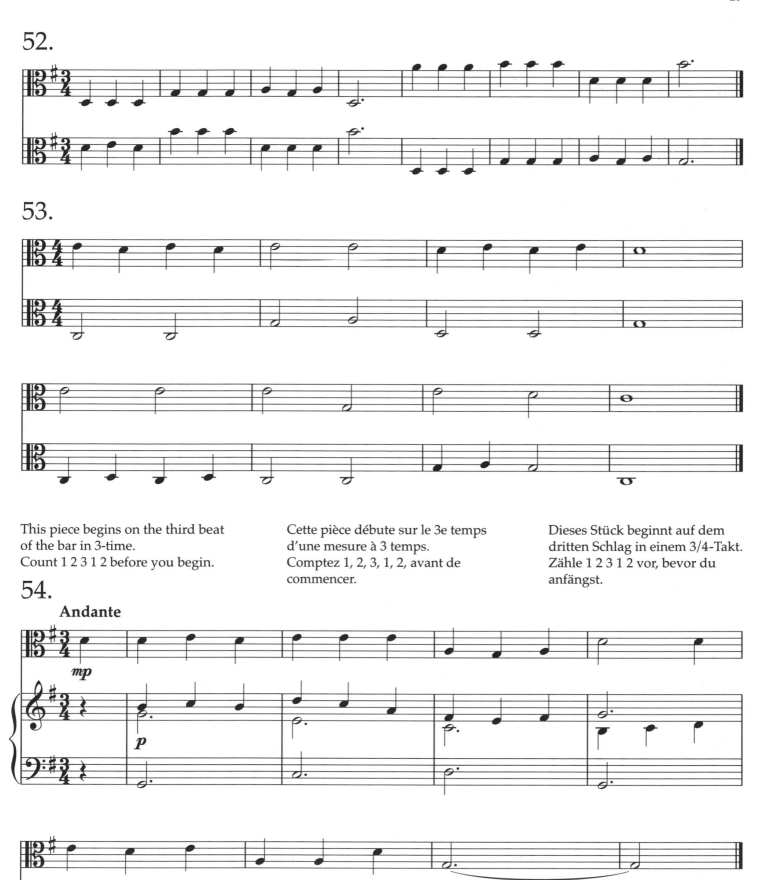

55.

Con moto

56.

Waltz

Section 3 – Adding the 2nd finger
Section 3 – Introduction du 2ème doigt
Teil 3 – Einführung des 2. Fingers

Five steps to success

1. **Look at the top number of the time signature**. Tap (clap, sing or play on one note) the rhythm, feeling the pulse throughout. Count at least one bar of the time signature in your head to set up the pulse before you tap or play.

2. **Look between the alto clef and the time signature for any sharps or flats**. Make sure you know which notes these apply to and notice where they occur in the melody.

3. **Look for patterns** in both the rhythms and in the melodic shape, and notice movement by step, skips, repeated notes and sequences.

4. **Identify the new fingers on the stave** and say the name of each note.

5. **Keep going!**

Cinq étapes vers la réussite

1. **Observez le chiffre supérieur de l'indication de mesure**. Frappez (dans les mains, chantez ou jouez sur une seule note) le rythme tout en maintenant une pulsation intérieure constante. Comptez mentalement au moins une mesure pour installer la pulsation avant de frapper ou de jouer chaque pièce.

2. **Vérifiez les dièses ou les bémols placés entre la clef d'ut 3e et les chiffres indicateurs de mesure**. Assurez-vous des notes altérées et repérez-les dans la mélodie.

3. **Repérez les motifs** rythmiques et mélodiques et relevez les déplacements par degrés, les sauts d'intervalles, les notes répétées et les séquences.

4. **Repérez les nouvelles positions des doigts et des notes sur la portée** et dites le nom de chaque note.

5. **Ne vous arrêtez pas !**

Fünf Schritte zum Erfolg

1. **Schaue dir die obere Zahl der Taktangabe an**. Schlage (klatsche, singe oder spiele auf einer Note) den Rhythmus, wobei du immer das Metrum spürst. Zähle mindestens einen Takt lang die Taktangabe im Kopf, um das Metrum zu verinnerlichen, bevor du klopfst oder spielst.

2. **Achte auf Kreuz- und B-Vorzeichen zwischen dem Notenschlüssel und der Taktangabe**. Überzeuge dich davon, dass du weißt, auf welche Noten sich diese beziehen und finde heraus, wo sie in der Melodie auftauchen.

3. **Achte auf Muster**: zum einen bei den Rhythmen und der melodischen Form, zum anderen bei Bewegungen in Schritten oder Sprüngen, sich wiederholende Noten und Sequenzen.

4. **Finde den neu hinzukommenden Finger im Notensystem** und sage den Namen jeder Note.

5. **Spiele immer weiter!**

Terms and performance directions used in the accompanied pieces:

Indications d'exécution utilisées dans les pièces accompagnées :

Begriffe und Vortragsangaben, die bei den begleiteten Stücken verwendet werden:

Andante	at a walking pace	allant	gehend
Dolce	sweetly	doux	süß
Moderato	at a moderate tempo	modéré	gemäßigt
Rit. (ritenuto)	gradually getting slower	en retenant progressivement le tempo	allmählich langsamer werdend
Waltz	a lively dance in 3-time	danse à trois temps	ein lebhafter Tanz im 3er-Takt

Section 3 – Adding the 2nd finger
Section 3 – Introduction du 2ème doigt
Teil 3 – Einführung des 2. Fingers

In this section, the 2nd finger will be one tone above the 1st finger.

Dans cette section le 2ème doigt jouera un ton au-dessus du premier.

In diesem Abschnitt wird der 2. Finger immer einen Ganzton über den 1. Finger gesetzt.

The key signature of C major.

Armure de la tonalité de *do* majeur.

Die Tonart C-Dur.

57.

The key signature of G major.

Armure de la tonalité de *sol* majeur.

Die Tonart G-Dur.

58.

The key signature of D major.

Armure de la tonalité de *ré* majeur.

Die Tonart D-Dur.

59.

D major.

ré majeur.

D-Dur.

60.

D major.

ré majeur.

D-Dur.

61.

G major.

sol majeur.

G-Dur.

62.

G major.   *sol* majeur.   G-Dur.

63.

D major.   *ré* majeur.   D-Dur.

64.

C major.   *do* majeur.   C-Dur.

65.

G major.   *sol* majeur.   G-Dur.

66.

G major.   *sol* majeur.   G-Dur.

67.

24

D major.   *ré* majeur.   D-Dur.

68.

C major.   *do* majeur.   C-Dur.

69.

70.

71.

72.

73.

74.

75.

Dolce

76.

Andante

77.

Moderato

78.

Waltz

Section 4 – Using the 3rd finger in major keys
Section 4 – Introduction du 3ème doigt dans les tonalités majeures
Teil 4 – Einführung des 3. Fingers in Dur-Tonarten

Five steps to success

1. **Look at the top number of the time signature**. Tap (clap, sing or play on one note) the rhythm, feeling the pulse throughout. Count at least one bar of the time signature in your head to set up the pulse before you tap or play.

2. **Look between the alto clef and the time signature for any sharps or flats**. Make sure you know which notes these apply to and notice where they occur in the melody.

3. **Look for patterns**. While tapping the rhythms, look at the melodic shape and notice movement by step, skips, repeated notes and sequences.

4. **Identify the new fingers on the stave** and say the name of each note.

5. **Keep going!**

Cinq étapes vers la réussite

1. **Observez le chiffre supérieur de l'indication de mesure**. Frappez (dans les mains, chantez ou jouez sur une seule note) le rythme tout en maintenant une pulsation intérieure constante. Comptez mentalement au moins une mesure pour installer la pulsation avant de frapper ou de jouer chaque pièce.

2. **Vérifiez les dièses ou les bémols placés entre la clef d'ut 3e et les chiffres indicateurs de mesure**. Assurez-vous des notes altérées et repérez-les dans la mélodie.

3. **Repérez les motifs**. Tout en frappant le rythme, observez les contours de la mélodie et relevez les déplacements par degrés, les sauts d'intervalles, les notes répétées et les séquences.

4. **Repérez les nouvelles positions des doigts et des notes sur la portée** et dites le nom de chaque note.

5. **Ne vous arrêtez pas !**

Fünf Schritte zum Erfolg

1. **Schaue dir die obere Zahl der Taktangabe an**. Schlage (klatsche, singe oder spiele auf einer Note) den Rhythmus, wobei du immer das Metrum spürst. Zähle mindestens einen Takt lang die Taktangabe im Kopf, um das Metrum zu verinnerlichen, bevor du klopfst oder spielst.

2. **Schaue zwischen den Notenschlüssel und die Taktangabe, um zu sehen, wie viele Vorzeichen die Tonart hat**. Überzeuge dich davon, dass du weißt, auf welche Noten sich diese beziehen und finde heraus, wo in der Melodie sie auftauchen.

3. **Achte auf Muster**. Schaue dir die melodische Form an, während du den Rhythmus schlägst und achte auf Bewegungen in Schritten oder Sprüngen, sich wiederholende Noten und Sequenzen.

4. **Finde den neu hinzukommenden Finger im Notensystem** und sage den Namen jeder Note.

5. **Spiele immer weiter!**

Terms and performance directions used in the duets and accompanied pieces:

Indications d'exécution utilisées dans les pièces accompagnées :

Begriffe und Vortragsangaben, die in den Duetten und begleiteten Stücken verwendet werden:

Allegretto	moderately fast	assez vite	gemäßigt schnell
Cantabile	in a singing style	chantant	gesanglich
Con moto	with vigour	avec force	mit Energie
Grazioso	gracefully	gracieux	anmutig
Maestoso	majestically	majestueux	majestätisch
Moderato	at a moderate tempo	modéré	gemäßigt
Vivace	lively	vif	lebhaft

Section 4 – Using the 3rd finger in major keys
Section 4 – Introduction du 3ème doigt dans les tonalités majeures
Teil 4 – Einführung des 3. Fingers in Dur-Tonarten

In this section, the 3rd finger always goes one semitone above the 2nd finger.

Clap and sing the following exercises before you play.

Dans cette section, le 3ème doigt joue toujours un demi-ton au-dessus du 2ème doigt.

Frappez dans les mains et chantez les exercices suivant avant de les jouer.

In diesem Abschnitt wird der 3. Finger immer einen Halbton über den 2. Finger gesetzt.

Klatsche und singe die folgenden Übungen bevor du anfängst.

C major.   *do* majeur.   C-Dur.

79.

G major.   *sol* majeur.   G-Dur.

80.

D major.   *ré* majeur.   D-Dur.

81.

A major.   *la* majeur.   A-Dur.

82.

Introducing quavers (eighth notes).

This piece begins on the third beat of the bar in 3-time.
Count 1 2 3 1 2 before you begin.

Introduction des croches.

Cette pièce débute sur le 3e temps d'une mesure à 3 temps.
Comptez 1, 2, 3, 1, 2, avant de commencer.

Einführung von Achteln.

Dieses Stück beginnt auf dem dritten Schlag in einem 3/4-Takt.
Zähle 1 2 3 1 2 vor, bevor du anfängst.

83.

This piece begins on the third beat of the bar in 3-time.
Count 1 2 3 1 2 before you begin.

Cette pièce débute sur le 3e temps d'une mesure à 3 temps.
Comptez 1, 2, 3, 1, 2, avant de commencer.

Dieses Stück beginnt auf dem dritten Schlag in einem 3/4-Takt.
Zähle 1 2 3 1 2 vor, bevor du anfängst.

84.

85.

86.

87.

This piece begins on the third beat of the bar in 3-time.
Count 1 2 3 1 2 before you begin.

Cette pièce débute sur le 3e temps d'une mesure à 3 temps.
Comptez 1, 2, 3, 1, 2, avant de commencer.

Dieses Stück beginnt auf dem dritten Schlag in einem 3/4-Takt.
Zähle 1 2 3 1 2 vor, bevor du anfängst.

88.

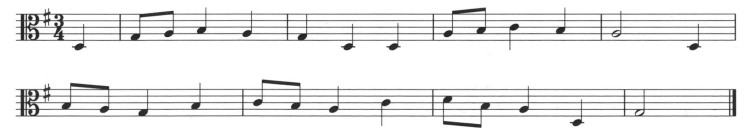

32

This piece begins on the third beat of the bar in 3-time.
Count 1 2 3 1 2 before you begin.

Cette pièce débute sur le 3e temps d'une mesure à 3 temps.
Comptez 1, 2, 3, 1, 2, avant de commencer.

Dieses Stück beginnt auf dem dritten Schlag in einem 3/4-Takt.
Zähle 1 2 3 1 2 vor, bevor du anfängst.

89.

90.

91.

Maestoso

92.

Grazioso

93.

Moderato

94.

Allegretto

95.

Vivace

This piece begins on the fourth beat of the bar in 4-time. Count 1 2 3 before you begin.

Cette pièce débute sur le 4e temps d'une mesure à 4 temps. Comptez 1, 2, 3, avant de commencer.

Dieses Stück beginnt auf dem vierten Schlag in einem 4/4-Takt. Zähle 1 2 3 vor, bevor du anfängst.

96.
Moderato

Slow waltz.   Valse lente.   Langsamer Walzer.

97.

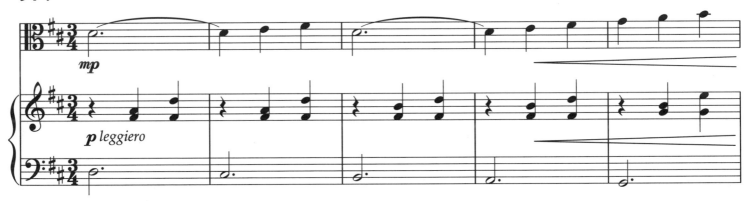

98.

Con moto

Section 5 – New keys: F major, B♭ major and E♭ major
Section 5 – Nouvelles tonalités : *fa* majeur, *si*♭ majeur et *mi*♭ majeur
Teil 5 – Neue Tonarten: F-Dur, B-Dur und Es-Dur

Five steps to success

1. **Look at the top number of the time signature**. Tap (clap, sing or play on one note) the rhythm, feeling the pulse throughout. Count at least one bar of the time signature in your head to set up the pulse before you begin.

2. **Look between the alto clef and the time signature**. You will see either one, two or three flats in the key signature or none at all. Learn these new keys and make sure you know which notes the new flats apply to and where they occur in the melody.

3. **Look for patterns**. While tapping the rhythms, look at the melodic shape and notice movement by step, skips, repeated notes and sequences.

4. **Be aware of the new notes and keys.**

5. **Keep going!**

Cinq étapes vers la réussite

1. **Observez le chiffre supérieur de l'indication de mesure**. Frappez (dans les mains, chantez ou jouez sur une seule note) le rythme tout en maintenant une pulsation intérieure constante. Comptez mentalement au moins une mesure pour installer la pulsation avant de frapper ou de jouer chaque pièce.

2. **Vérifiez l'armure placée entre la clef d'ut 3e et les chiffres indicateurs de mesure**. Vous constaterez la présence d'un, deux ou trois bémols ou d'aucun bémol à l'armure de la clef. Apprenez ces nouvelles tonalités et assurez-vous de connaître les notes bémolisées et de les repérer dans la mélodie.

3. **Repérez les motifs**. Tout en frappant les rythmes, observez les contours de la mélodie et relevez les déplacements par degrés, les sauts d'intervalles, les notes répétées et les séquences.

4. **Repérez les nouvelles notes et tonalités.**

5. **Ne vous arrêtez pas !**

Fünf Schritte zum Erfolg

1. **Schau dir die obere Zahl der Taktangabe an**. Schlage (klatsche, singe oder spiele auf einer Note) den Rhythmus, wobei du immer das Metrum spürst. Zähle mindestens einen Takt lang die Taktangabe im Kopf, um das Metrum zu verinnerlichen, bevor du klopfst oder spielst.

2. **Schaue zwischen Notenschlüssel und Taktangabe**. Du wirst entweder ein, zwei, drei oder gar kein B-Vorzeichen finden. Lerne sie und überzeuge dich davon, dass du weißt, auf welche Noten sich diese neuen B-Vorzeichen beziehen und wo sie in der Melodie auftauchen.

3. **Achte auf Muster**. Schaue dir die melodische Form an, während du den Rhythmus schlägst und achte auf Bewegungen in Schritten oder Sprüngen, sich wiederholende Noten und Sequenzen.

4. **Sei dir der neuen Noten und Vorzeichen bewusst.**

5. **Spiele immer weiter!**

Terms and performance directions used in the duets and accompanied pieces:

Termes et indications d'exécution utilisés dans les duos et les pièces accompagnées :

Begriffe und Vortragsangaben, die in den Duetten und begleiteten Stücken verwendet werden:

Allegro ma non troppo	fast, but not too fast	rapide mais pas trop	schnell, aber nicht zu schnell
Andante	at a walking pace	allant	gehend
Con moto	with vigour	avec force	mit Bewegung
Dolce	sweetly	doux	süß
Grazioso	gracefully	gracieux	anmutig
Maestoso	majestically	majestueux	majestätisch
Moderato	at a moderate tempo	modéré	gemäßigt
Poco	a little	un peu	ein wenig
Poco adagio	a little slowly	un peu lent	ein wenig langsam

Section 5 – New keys: F major, B♭ major and E♭ major
Section 5 – Nouvelles tonalités : *fa* majeur, *si*♭ majeur et
mi♭ majeur

Teil 5 – Neue Tonarten: F-Dur, B-Dur und Es-Dur

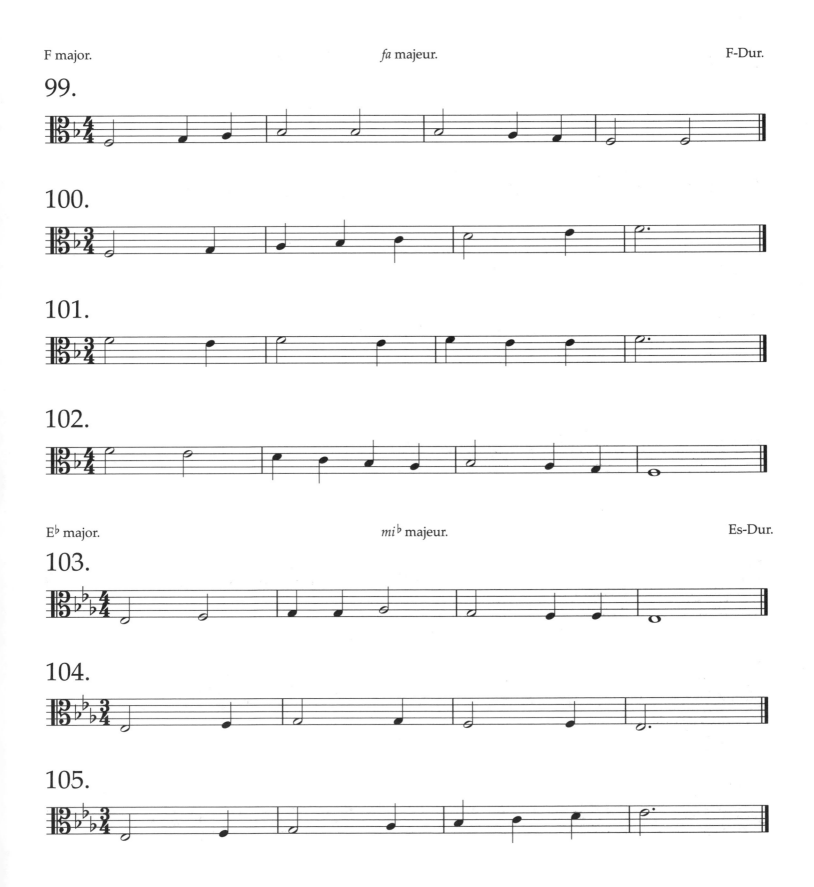

106.

B♭ major.   *si*♭ majeur.   B-Dur.

107.

108.

Mixed keys.   Tonalités diverses.   Verschiedene Tonarten.

109.

110.

111.

112.

113.

114.

115.

116.

117.

This piece begins on the fourth beat of the bar in 4-time. Count 1 2 3 before you begin.

Cette pièce débute sur le 4e temps d'une mesure à 4 temps. Comptez 1, 2, 3, avant de commencer.

Dieses Stück beginnt auf dem vierten Schlag in einem 4/4-Takt. Zähle 1 2 3 vor, bevor du anfängst.

118.

This piece begins on the third beat of the bar in 3-time. Count 1 2 3 1 2 before you begin.

Cette pièce débute sur le 3e temps d'une mesure à 3 temps. Comptez 1, 2, 3, 1, 2, avant de commencer.

Dieses Stück beginnt auf dem dritten Schlag in einem 3/4-Takt. Zähle 1 2 3 1 2 vor, bevor du anfängst.

119.

120.

Poco adagio

121.

Con moto

122.

Maestoso

This piece begins on the third beat of the bar in 3-time.	Cette pièce débute sur le 3e temps d'une mesure à 3 temps.	Dieses Stück beginnt auf dem dritten Schlag in einem 3/4-Takt.
Count 1 2 3 1 2 before you begin.	Comptez 1, 2, 3, 1, 2, avant de commencer.	Zähle 1 2 3 1 2 vor, bevor du anfängst.

123.

Grazioso

124.

Allegro ma non troppo

This piece begins on the third beat
of the bar in 3-time.
Count 1 2 3 1 2 before you begin.

Cette pièce débute sur le 3e temps
d'une mesure à 3 temps.
Comptez 1, 2, 3, 1, 2, avant de
commencer.

Dieses Stück beginnt auf dem
dritten Schlag in einem 3/4-Takt.
Zähle 1 2 3 1 2 vor, bevor du
anfängst.

125.

Andante

126.

Moderato

This piece begins on the third beat
of the bar in 3-time.
Count 1 2 3 1 2 before you begin.

Cette pièce débute sur le 3e temps
d'une mesure à 3 temps.
Comptez 1, 2, 3, 1, 2, avant de
commencer.

Dieses Stück beginnt auf dem
dritten Schlag in einem 3/4-Takt.
Zähle 1 2 3 1 2 vor, bevor du
anfängst.

127.

Moderato

128.

Quick waltz.   Valse rapide.   Schneller Walzer.

129.

Section 6 – New rhythms and slurs
Section 6 – Nouveaux rythmes et liaisons de phrasé
Teil 6 – Neue Rhythmen und Bindungen

Five steps to success

1. **Look at the top number of the time signature**. Tap (clap, sing or play on one note) the rhythm, feeling the pulse throughout. Count at least one bar of the time signature in your head to set up the pulse before you tap or play.

2. **Look between the alto clef and the time signature for any sharps or flats**. This is known as the key signature. Make sure you know which notes these apply to and where they occur in the melody.

3. **Look for patterns**. While tapping the rhythm, look at the melodic shape and notice movement by step, skips, repeated notes and sequences.

4. **Notice the articulation and dynamics**. Observe the dynamic shape and notice if the changes are sudden or gradual.

5. **Keep going!**

Cinq étapes vers la réussite

1. **Observez l'indication de mesure**. Frappez (dans les mains, chantez ou jouez sur une seule note) le rythme tout en maintenant une pulsation intérieure constante. Comptez mentalement au moins une mesure pour installer la pulsation avant de frapper le rythme ou de jouer la pièce.

2. **Vérifiez les dièses et les bémols placés entre la clef d'ut 3e et l'indication de mesure**. Ils constituent l'armure de la tonalité. Assurez-vous des notes altérées et repérez-les dans la mélodie.

3. **Repérez les motifs**. Tout en frappant le rythme, observez les contours de la mélodie et relevez les mouvements par degré, les sauts d'intervalles, les notes répétées et les séquences.

4. **Observez le phrasé et les nuances**. Examinez les formes dynamiques et notez leurs changements subits ou progressifs.

5. **Ne vous arrêtez pas !**

Fünf Schritte zum Erfolg

1. **Schaue dir die obere Zahl der Taktangabe an**. Schlage (klatsche, singe oder spiele auf einer Note) den Rhythmus, wobei du immer das Metrum spürst. Zähle mindestens einen Takt lang die Taktangabe im Kopf, um das Metrum zu verinnerlichen, bevor du klopfst oder spielst.

2. **Schaue zwischen Notenschlüssel und Taktangabe nach Kreuz- oder B-Vorzeichen**. Diese ergeben die Tonart.Vergewissere dich, dass du weißt, auf welche Noten sie sich beziehen und wo sie in der Melodie auftauchen.

3. **Achte auf Muster**. Schaue dir die melodische Form an, während du den Rhythmus schlägst und achte auf Bewegungen in Schritten oder Sprüngen, sich wiederholende Noten und Sequenzen.

4. **Beachte Artikulation und Dynamik**. Schaue die Dynamikzeichen genau an und erkenne, ob die Veränderungen plötzlich oder allmählich sind.

5. **Spiele immer weiter!**

Terms and performance directions used in this section:

Termes et indications d'exécutions utilisés dans cette section :

Begriffe und Vortragsangaben, die in diesem Teil verwendet werden:

Adagio	slowly	lent	langsam
Andante	at a walking pace	allant	gehend
Andantino	a little faster than Andante	un peu plus vite qu'Andante	ein bisschen schneller als Andante
Allegretto	moderately fast	assez rapide	gemäßigt schnell
Con grazia	with grace	avec grâce	mit Anmut
Con moto	with vigour	avec force	mit Energie
Dolce	sweetly	doux	süß
Gavotte	a lively dance beginning of the 3rd beat	danse vive commençant sur le 3ème temps	ein lebhafter Tanz, der auf dem dritten Schlag beginnt
Grazioso	gracefully	gracieux	anmutig
Maestoso	majestically	majestueux	majestätisch
Mesto	sadly	triste	traurig
Moderato	at a moderate tempo	modéré	gemäßigt
Poco adagio	a little slowly	un peu lent	ein wenig langsam
Poco allegro	a little fast	un peu rapide	ein wenig schnell
Poco lento	a little slowly	un peu lent	ein wenig langsam
Risoluto	resolutely	résolu	entschieden
Ritmico	rhythmically	rythmique	rhythmisch
Subito (*sub.*)	suddenly	soudain	plötzlich
Tranquillo	tranquil	tranquille	ruhig
Vivace	lively	vif	lebhaft
Vivo	lively	vif	lebhaft

Section 6 – New rhythms and slurs
Section 6 – Nouveaux rythmes et liaisons de phrasé
Teil 6 – Neue Rhythmen und Bindungen

130.

Andante

131.

Poco lento

This piece begins on the second beat of the bar in 2-time. Count 1 2 1 before you begin.	Cette pièce débute sur le 2e temps d'une mesure à 2 temps. Comptez 1, 2, 1, avant de commencer.	Dieses Stück beginnt auf dem zweiten Schlag in einem 2/4-Takt. Zähle 1 2 1 vor, bevor du anfängst.

132.

Vivo

This piece begins on the second beat of the bar in 2-time. Count 1 2 1 before you begin.	Cette pièce débute sur le 2e temps d'une mesure à 2 temps. Comptez 1, 2, 1, avant de commencer.	Dieses Stück beginnt auf dem zweiten Schlag in einem 2/4-Takt. Zähle 1 2 1 vor, bevor du anfängst.

133.

Allegretto

134.

Poco allegro

135.

Con grazia

Adding slurs.   Introduction des liaisons de phrasé.   Einführung von Bindungen.

136.
Dolce

137.
Moderato

138.
Vivace

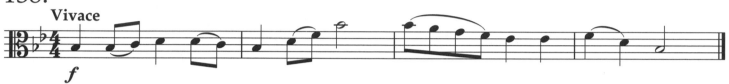

139.
Andantino

140.
Risoluto

141.
Maestoso

142.
Ritmico

143.
Moderato

144.

Andantino

Minor keys. Tonalités mineures. Moll-Tonarten.
C minor. *do* mineur. c-Moll.

145.

Poco adagio

146.

Moderato

G minor. *sol* mineur. g-Moll.

147.

Allegretto

148.

Andante

D minor. *ré* mineur. d-Moll.

149.

Grazioso

150.

Ritmico

151.

Con grazia

This piece begins on the third beat of the bar in 3-time.
Count 1 2 3 1 2 before you begin.

Cette pièce débute sur le 3e temps d'une mesure à 3 temps.
Comptez 1, 2, 3, 1, 2, avant de commencer.

Dieses Stück beginnt auf dem dritten Schlag in einem 3/4-Takt.
Zähle 1 2 3 1 2 vor, bevor du anfängst.

152.

Con moto

This piece begins on the fourth beat of the bar in 4-time.
Count 1 2 3 before you begin.

Cette pièce débute sur le 4e temps d'une mesure à 4 temps.
Comptez 1, 2, 3, avant de commencer.

Dieses Stück beginnt auf dem vierten Schlag in einem 4/4-Takt.
Zähle 1 2 3 vor, bevor du anfängst.

153.

Con moto

This piece begins on the third beat of the bar in 3-time.
Count 1 2 3 1 2 before you begin.

Cette pièce débute sur le 3e temps d'une mesure à 3 temps.
Comptez 1, 2, 3, 1, 2, avant de commencer.

Dieses Stück beginnt auf dem dritten Schlag in einem 3/4-Takt.
Zähle 1 2 3 1 2 vor, bevor du anfängst.

154. Grazioso

155. Poco lento

156. Moderato

157.

Tranquillo

mp

158.

Adagio

p

This piece begins on the third beat of the bar in 3-time. Count 1 2 3 1 2 before you begin.	Cette pièce débute sur le 3e temps d'une mesure à 3 temps. Comptez 1, 2, 3, 1, 2, avant de commencer.	Dieses Stück beginnt auf dem dritten Schlag in einem 3/4-Takt. Zähle 1 2 3 1 2 vor, bevor du anfängst.

159.

Andante

mp   *f*   *mp*

This piece begins on the third beat of the bar in 4-time. Count 1 2 3 4 1 2 before you begin.	Cette pièce débute sur le 3e temps d'une mesure à 4 temps. Comptez 1, 2, 3, 4, 1, 2, avant de commencer.	Dieses Stück beginnt auf dem dritten Schlag in einem 4/4-Takt. Zähle 1 2 3 4 1 2 vor, bevor du anfängst.

160.

Gavotte

f   *mf*   *f*

This piece begins on the fourth
beat of the bar in 4-time.
Count 1 2 3 before you begin.

Cette pièce débute sur le 4e temps
d'une mesure à 4 temps.
Comptez 1, 2, 3, avant de commencer.

Dieses Stück beginnt auf dem
vierten Schlag in einem 4/4-Takt.
Zähle 1 2 3 vor, bevor du anfängst.

161.

Maestoso

This piece begins on the fourth
beat of the bar in 4-time.
Count 1 2 3 before you begin.

Cette pièce débute sur le 4e temps
d'une mesure à 4 temps.
Comptez 1, 2, 3, avant de commencer.

Dieses Stück beginnt auf dem
vierten Schlag in einem 4/4-Takt.
Zähle 1 2 3 vor, bevor du anfängst.

162.

Mesto

163.

This piece begins on the fourth beat of the bar in 4-time. Count 1 2 3 before you begin.

Cette pièce débute sur le 4e temps d'une mesure à 4 temps. Comptez 1, 2, 3, avant de commencer.

Dieses Stück beginnt auf dem vierten Schlag in einem 4/4-Takt. Zähle 1 2 3 vor, bevor du anfängst.

164.

Vivace

Section 7 – Counting quaver beats in 3/8 time
Section 7 – Battue des croches dans la mesure à 3/8
Teil 7 – Das Zählen von Achtelschlägen im 3/8-Takt

Six steps to success

1. **Look at the top number of the time signature**. Tap (clap, sing or play on one note) the rhythm, feeling the pulse throughout. Count at least one bar in your head to set up the tempo before you tap or play.

2. **Look between the alto clef and the time signature for any sharps or flats**. This is the key signature. Make sure you know which notes these apply to and where they occur in the melody.

3. **Look for patterns**. While tapping the rhythm, look at the melodic shape and notice movement by step, skips, repeated notes and sequences.

4. **Look out for accidentals**. You will need to watch out for additional sharps, flats or naturals, particularly when playing in minor keys.

5. **Notice the articulation and dynamics**.

6. **Keep going!**

Six étapes vers la réussite

1. **Observez l'indication de mesure**. Frappez (dans les mains, chantez ou jouez sur une seule note) le rythme tout en maintenant une pulsation intérieure constante. Comptez mentalement au moins une mesure pour installer la pulsation avant de frapper le rythme ou de jouer la pièce.

2. **Vérifiez les dièses ou les bémols placés entre la clef d'ut 3e et l'indication de mesure**. Ils constituent l'armure de la tonalité. Assurez-vous des notes altérées et repérez-les dans la mélodie.

3. **Repérez les motifs**. Tout en frappant le rythme, observez les contours de la mélodie et relevez les mouvements par degré, les sauts d'intervalles, les notes répétées et les séquences.

4. **Recherchez les altérations accidentelles**. Soyez attentifs aux dièses, bémols ou bécarres ajoutés, en particulier dans les tonalités mineures.

5. **Observez le phrasé et les nuances**.

6. **Ne vous arrêtez pas !**

Sechs Schritte zum Erfolg

1. **Schaue dir die obere Zahl der Taktangabe an**. Schlage (klatsche, singe oder spiele auf einer Note) den Rhythmus, wobei du immer das Metrum spürst. Zähle mindestens einen Takt lang die Taktangabe im Kopf, um das Metrum zu verinnerlichen, bevor du klopfst oder spielst.

2. **Schaue zwischen Notenschlüssel und Taktangabe nach Kreuz- oder B-Vorzeichen**. Diese zeigen die Tonart an. Vergewissere dich, dass du weißt, auf welche Noten sie sich beziehen und wo sie in der Melodie auftauchen.

3. **Achte auf Muster**. Schaue dir die melodische Form an, während du den Rhythmus schlägst und achte auf Bewegungen in Schritten oder Sprüngen, sich wiederholende Noten und Sequenzen.

4. **Suche nach Vorzeichen im Stück**. Du musst nach zusätzlichen Kreuzen, Bs oder Auflösungszeichen Ausschau halten, besonders bei den Stücken, die in einer Molltonart stehen.

5. **Beachte Artikulation und Dynamik**.

6. **Spiele immer weiter!**

Terms and performance directions used in the duets and accompanied pieces:

Termes et indications d'exécution utilisés dans les duos et les pièces avec accompagnement :

Begriffe und Vortragsangaben, die in den Duetten und begleiteten Stücken verwendet werden:

Allegro vivace	fast and lively	rapide et vif	schnell und lebhaft
Andante sostenuto	at a walking pace and sustained	allant et soutenu	gehend und zurückhaltend
Mesto	sadly	triste	traurig
Mesto sostenuto	sadly and sustained	triste et soutenu	traurig und zurückhaltend
Poco lento	a little slowly	un peu lent	ein wenig langsam
Risoluto	resolutely	résolu	entschieden
Sostenuto	sustained	soutenu	zurückhaltend
Vivace	lively	vif	lebhaft

Section 7 – Counting quaver beats in 3/8 time

Section 7 – Battue des croches dans la mesure à 3/8

Teil 7 – Das Zählen von Achtelschlägen im 3/8-Takt

Play these at a moderate tempo, counting 1 2 3 throughout.

Jouer ces pièces à une allure modérée et sans cesser de compter 1, 2, 3.

Spiele diese Stücke in einem mäßigen Tempo und zähle 1 2 3.

165.

166.

167.

168.

169.

170.

171.

Shifts.   Déplacements.   Lagenwechsel.

172.

173.

174.

175.

176.

This piece begins on the fourth beat of the bar in 4-time.
Count 1 2 3 before you begin.

Cette pièce débute sur le 4e temps d'une mesure à 4 temps.
Comptez 1, 2, 3, avant de commencer.

Dieses Stück beginnt auf dem vierten Schlag in einem 4/4-Takt.
Zähle 1 2 3 vor, bevor du anfängst.

177.

This piece begins on the third beat of the bar in 3-time.
Count 1 2 3 1 2 before you begin.

Cette pièce débute sur le 3e temps d'une mesure à 3 temps.
Comptez 1, 2, 3, 1, 2, avant de commencer.

Dieses Stück beginnt auf dem dritten Schlag in einem 3/4-Takt.
Zähle 1 2 3 1 2 vor, bevor du anfängst.

178.

179.

180.

181.

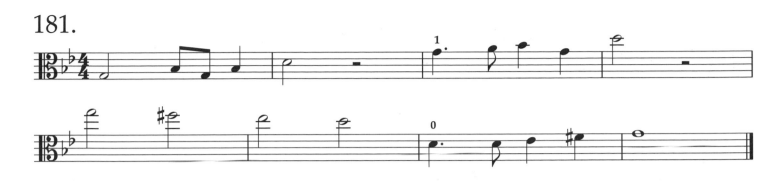

This piece begins on the third beat of the bar in 3-time.
Count 1 2 3 1 2 before you begin.

Cette pièce débute sur le 3e temps d'une mesure à 3 temps.
Comptez 1, 2, 3, 1, 2, avant de commencer.

Dieses Stück beginnt auf dem dritten Schlag in einem 3/4-Takt.
Zähle 1 2 3 1 2 vor, bevor du anfängst.

182.

183.

This piece begins on the third beat of the bar in 3-time.
Count 1 2 3 1 2 before you begin.

Cette pièce débute sur le 3e temps d'une mesure à 3 temps.
Comptez 1, 2, 3, 1, 2, avant de commencer.

Dieses Stück beginnt auf dem dritten Schlag in einem 3/4-Takt.
Zähle 1 2 3 1 2 vor, bevor du anfängst.

184.

185.

186.

187.

Poco lento

188.

Vivace

189.

Sostenuto

This piece begins on the third beat of the bar in 3-time.
Count 1 2 3 1 2 before you begin.

Cette pièce débute sur le 3e temps d'une mesure à 3 temps.
Comptez 1, 2, 3, 1, 2, avant de commencer.

Dieses Stück beginnt auf dem dritten Schlag in einem 3/8-Takt.
Zähle 1 2 3 1 2 vor, bevor du anfängst.

190.

Risoluto

191.

Vivace

192.

Allegro vivace

This piece begins on the third beat of the bar in 3-time.
Count 1 2 3 1 2 before you begin.

Cette pièce débute sur le 3e temps d'une mesure à 3 temps.
Comptez 1, 2, 3, 1, 2, avant de commencer.

Dieses Stück beginnt auf dem dritten Schlag in einem 3/8-Takt.
Zähle 1 2 3 1 2 vor, bevor du anfängst.

193.

Mesto

194.

Mesto sostenuto

This piece begins on the third beat
of the bar in 3-time.
Count 1 2 3 1 2 before you begin.

Cette pièce débute sur le 3e temps
d'une mesure à 3 temps.
Comptez 1, 2, 3, 1, 2, avant de
commencer.

Dieses Stück beginnt auf dem
dritten Schlag in einem 3/8-Takt.
Zähle 1 2 3 1 2 vor, bevor du
anfängst.

195.

Vivace

64

196.

Andante sostenuto

Section 8 – Compound time
Section 8 – Mesures composées
Teil 8 – Zusammengesetzte Taktarten

Six steps to success

1. **Look at the top number of the time signature**. Tap (clap, sing or play on one note) the rhythm, feeling the pulse throughout. Count at least one bar in your head to set up the tempo before you tap or play.

2. **Look between the alto clef and the time signature for any sharps or flats**. This is the key signature. Make sure you know which notes these apply to and where they occur in the melody.

3. **Look for patterns**. While tapping the rhythm, look at the melodic shape and notice movement by step, skips, repeated notes and sequences.

4. **Look for accidentals**. You will need to watch for additional sharps, flats or naturals, particularly when playing in minor keys.

5. **Notice the articulation and dynamics**. Observe the dynamic shape and note whether the changes are sudden or gradual.

6. **Keep going!**

Six étapes vers la réussite

1. **Observez l'indication de mesure**. Frappez (dans les mains, chantez ou jouez sur une seule note) le rythme tout en maintenant une pulsation intérieure constante. Comptez mentalement au moins une mesure pour installer la pulsation avant de frapper le rythme ou de jouer la pièce.

2. **Vérifiez les dièses ou les bémols placés entre la clef d'ut 3e et l'indication de mesure**. Ils constituent l'armure de la tonalité. Assurez-vous des notes altérées et repérez-les dans la mélodie.

3. **Repérez les motifs**. Tout en frappant le rythme, observez les contours de la mélodie et relevez les mouvements par degré, les sauts d'intervalles, les notes répétées et les séquences.

4. **Recherchez les altérations accidentelles**. Soyez attentifs aux dièses, bémols ou bécarres ajoutés, en particulier dans les tonalités mineures.

5. **Observez le phrasé et les nuances**. Examinez les formes dynamiques et notez leurs changements subits ou progressifs.

6. **Ne vous arrêtez pas !**

Sechs Schritte zum Erfolg

1. **Schaue dir die obere Zahl der Taktangabe an**. Schlage (klatsche, singe oder spiele auf einer Note) den Rhythmus, wobei du immer das Metrum spürst. Zähle mindestens einen Takt lang die Taktangabe im Kopf, um das Metrum zu verinnerlichen, bevor du klopfst oder spielst.

2. **Schaue zwischen Notenschlüssel und Taktangabe nach Kreuz- oder B-Vorzeichen**. Diese zeigen die Tonart an. Vergewissere dich, dass du weißt, auf welche Noten sie sich beziehen und wo sie in der Melodie auftauchen.

3. **Achte auf Muster**. Schaue dir die melodische Form an, während du den Rhythmus schlägst und achte auf Bewegungen in Schritten oder Sprüngen, sich wiederholende Noten und Sequenzen.

4. **Suche nach Vorzeichen im Stück**. Du musst nach zusätzlichen Kreuzen, Bs oder Auflösungszeichen Ausschau halten, besonders bei den Stücken, die in einer Molltonart stehen.

5. **Beachte Artikulation und Dynamik**. Schaue die Dynamikzeichen genau an und erkenne, ob die Veränderungen plötzlich oder allmählich sind.

6. **Spiele immer weiter!**

New terms and performance directions used in this section:

Nouveaux termes et indications d'exécution utilisés dans cette section :

Neue Begriffe und Vortragsangaben, die in diesem Teil verwendet werden:

Barcarolle	a 'boat song' derived from the Venetian Gondoliers	chant de gondoliers	ein „Bootslied", das von den venetianischen Gondoliere abstammt
Crescendo (*cresc.*)	growing louder	en croissant	anwachsend
Energetico	energetically	énergique	voller Energie
Simile (*sim.*)	similar	semblable	ähnlich
Tarantella	a lively dance from Taranto in southern Italy – supposedly a cure for the bite of the tarantula!	Tarentelle, danse originaire de Tarente dans le sud de l'Italie, supposée guérir des morsures d'araignées (*tarantula*)	ein lebhafter Tanz aus Tarent in Süditalien; angeblich ein Heilmittel gegen den Biß der Tarantel!

Key steps to understanding compound rhythms

1. 6/8, 9/8 and 12/8 are known as 'compound' time signatures. Each beat is divided into three equal parts (say the word 'elephant' to a beat), unlike with 'simple' time signatures (2/4, 3/4 and 4/4), where the beat is divided into two equal parts (say the word 'tiger' to a beat).

2. 6/8 is the most common of these time signatures and means six equal quavers (eighth notes) in a bar. In 6/8 there are two groups of three quavers (eighth notes) so each bar has two beats and will be counted in two.

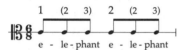

3. The opening bars of 'Humpty Dumpty' contain three of the most common rhythms encountered in compound time.

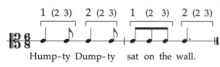

4. In all compound time signatures

♩. = two beats

♩. = one beat

♩ = two thirds of a beat

♪ = one third of a beat

5.
6/8 is two beats in a bar (two groups of three quavers)

9/8 is three beats in a bar (three groups of three quavers)

12/8 is four beats in a bar (four groups of three quavers)

Etapes essentielles à la compréhension des mesures composées

1. 6/8, 9/8 et 12/8 constituent les indications de mesures composées. Chaque temps y est divisé en trois parties égales (prononcez le mot « éléphant » sur chaque temps) à la différence des mesures simples (2/4, 3/4, et 4/4) dont les temps se divisent en deux parties égales (prononcez les mot « canard » sur chaque temps).

2. 6/8 est l'indication de mesure composée la plus fréquente et signifie que chaque mesure contient six croches égales. Chaque mesure à 6/8 contient deux groupes de trois croches. C'est donc une mesure à deux temps.

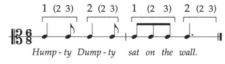

3. Les deux premières mesures de *Humpty Dumpty* présentent les trois rythmes les plus fréquemment rencontrés dans les mesures composées.

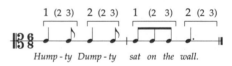

4. Dans toutes les mesures composées

♩. = deux temps

♩. = un temps

♩ = deux tiers de temps

♪ = un tiers de temps

5.
6/8 indique deux temps par mesure (deux groupes de trois croches)

9/8 indique trois temps par mesure (trois groupes de trois croches)

12/8 indique quatre temps par mesure (quatre groupes de trois croches)

Die entscheidenden Schritte, um zusammengesetzte Taktarten zu verstehen

1. 6/8-, 9/8- und 12/8-Takte sind als zusammengesetzte Taktarten bekannt. Jeder Schlag ist in drei gleichlange Teile aufgeteilt (sage das Wort „Murmeltier" auf einen Schlag) im Gegensatz zu einfachen Taktarten (2/4, 3/4 und 4/4), bei denen der Grundschlag in zwei gleichlange Teile unterteilt ist (sage das Wort „Tiger" auf einen Schlag).

2. Von diesen Taktarten kommt der 6/8-Takt am häufigsten vor. Er besteht aus sechs gleichlangen Achteln in einem Takt. Im 6/8-Takt gibt es zwei Gruppen mit je drei Achtelnoten. Jeder Takt hat also zwei Schläge und wird auf „zwei" gezählt.

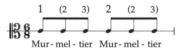

3. Die Eröffnungstakte des Kinderliedes *Humpty Dumpty* beinhalten die drei häufigsten Rhythmen, die man in zusammengesetzten Taktarten finden kann.

4. In allen zusammengesetzten Taktarten sind

♩. = zwei Schläge

♩. = ein Schlag

♩ = 2/3 eines Schlages

♪ = 1/3 eines Schlages

5.
6/8 hat zwei Schläge in einem Takt (zwei Gruppen mit drei Achteln)

9/8 hat drei Schläge in einem Takt (drei Gruppen mit drei Achteln)

12/8 hat vier Schläge in einem Takt (vier Gruppen mit drei Achteln)

Section 8 – Compound time
Section 8 – Mesures composées
Teil 8 – Zusammengesetzte Taktarten

197.

Andante

198.

Vivo

This piece begins after the second beat of the bar in 2-time. Count 1 (2 3) 2 (2) before you begin.	Cette pièce débute après le 2e temps d'une mesure à 2 temps. Comptez 1 (2, 3), 2 (2) avant de commencer.	Dieses Stück beginnt auf dem letzten Achtel in einem 6/8-Takt. Zähle 1 (2 3) 2 (2) vor, bevor du anfängst.

199.

Energetico

This piece begins on the sixth quaver of the bar in 2-time. At this tempo count 1 (2 3) 4 (5) before you begin.	Cette pièce débute sur la sixième croche d'une mesure à 2 temps. Comptez 1 (2, 3), 4 (5) à ce tempo avant de commencer.	Dieses Stück beginnt auf dem letzten Achtel in einem 6/8-Takt. Zähle auf Grund des langsamen Tempos 1 (2 3) 4 (5) vor, bevor du anfängst.

200.

Adagio

201.

Moderato

202.

Poco lento

This piece begins after the second beat of the bar in 2-time.
Count 1 (2 3) 2 (2) before you begin.

Cette pièce débute après le 2e temps d'une mesure à 2 temps.
Comptez 1 (2, 3), 2 (2) avant de commencer.

Dieses Stück beginnt auf dem letzten Achtel in einem 6/8-Takt.
Zähle 1 (2 3) 2 (2) vor, bevor du anfängst.

203.

Allegretto

204.

Ritmico

205.

Andante

206.

Allegro

This piece begins after the third beat of the bar in 3-time.
Count 1 (2 3) 2 (2 3) 3 (2) before you begin.

Cette pièce débute après le 3e temps d'une mesure à 3 temps.
Comptez 1 (2, 3), 2 (2, 3), 3 (2) avant de commencer.

Dieses Stück beginnt auf dem letzten Achtel in einem 9/8-Takt.
Zähle 1 (2 3) 2 (2 3) 3 (2) vor, bevor du anfängst.

207.

208.

This piece begins after the third beat of the bar in 3-time.
Count 1 (2 3) 2 (2 3) 3 (2) before you begin.

Cette pièce débute après le 3e temps d'une mesure à 3 temps.
Comptez 1 (2, 3), 2 (2, 3), 3 (2) avant de commencer.

Dieses Stück beginnt auf dem letzten Achtel in einem 9/8-Takt.
Zähle 1 (2 3) 2 (2 3) 3 (2) vor, bevor du anfängst.

209.

This piece begins after the third beat of the bar in 3-time.
Count 1 (2 3) 2 (2 3) 3 (2) before you begin.

Cette pièce débute après le 3e temps d'une mesure à 3 temps.
Comptez 1 (2, 3), 2 (2, 3), 3 (2) avant de commencer.

Dieses Stück beginnt auf dem letzten Achtel in einem 9/8-Takt.
Zähle 1 (2 3) 2 (2 3) 3 (2) vor, bevor du anfängst.

210.

212.

72

The last note in this piece is to
be plucked with the left hand.

La dernière note de cette pièce
sera pincée de la main gauche.

Die letzte Note in diesem Stück
wird mit der linken Hand gezupft.

213.

214.

Glossary
Glossaire
Glossar

Note performance directions together with their translations used throughout the book so that you have a complete list. Writing them down will help you to remember them.

Inscrivez ici les indications d'exécution utilisées dans ce volume et leur traduction pour en établir une liste complète. Le fait de les noter vous aidera à les retenir.

Schreibe hier alle Vortragsangaben, die im Buch verwendet werden, zusammen mit ihren Übersetzungen auf, so dass du eine vollständige Liste hast. Das Aufschreiben wird dir dabei helfen sie einzuprägen.

Adagio	Slowly	Lent	Langsam